WomensWords

A Woman's Prerogative

Edited by

Heather Killingray

First published in Great Britain in 1998 by
WOMENSWORDS
1-2 Wainman Road, Woodston,
Peterborough, PE2 7BU
Telephone (01733) 230746
Fax (01733) 230751

HB ISBN 0 75430 552 X
SB ISBN 0 75430 553 8

FOREWORD

Although we are a nation of poetry writers we are accused of not reading poetry and not buying poetry books: after many years of listening to the incessant gripes of poetry publishers, I can only assume that the books they publish, in general, are books that most people do not want to read.

Poetry should not be obscure, introverted, and as cryptic as a crossword puzzle: it is the poet's duty to reach out and embrace the world.

The world owes the poet nothing and we should not be expected to dig and delve into a rambling discourse searching for some inner meaning.

The reason we write poetry (and almost all of us do) is because we want to communicate: an ideal; an idea; or a specific feeling. Poetry is as essential in communication, as a letter; a radio; a telephone, and the main criteria for selecting the poems in this anthology is very simple: they communicate.

Heather Killingray
Editor

CONTENTS

MY FACE

This isn't me
This face I see
When I look in the mirror each day.

This can't be me
This face I see
I'm not old, or lined, or grey.

The face I see
Living inside me
Is young, unlined and gay.

What a pity it be
No-one else can see
The beautiful face that's inside me.

E Torkington

THE LOST FRIENDS

In France or in Bicester, Didcot or Barnes,
Sailing with Greeks on a shrimp catcher's barge,
Buried in a churchyard, Highgate by the spire,
Dancing with sailors or dancing with fire.

Sitting in Stepney, ringing a bell,
Watching for signs of the horned one from Hell.
Looking for Palestine, lost in the past,
Chasing wet froth up a seafarer's mast.

Living in Luton at Flat Thirteen A,
Bringing up children all through the day.
Selling insurance from door front to door,
Selling your services fleshy and raw.

Advising old men how to settle their wills,
Prescribing placebos for those who love pills.
Translating in Munich, for British MPs,
Or scrubbing out lavatories down on your knees.

The lost friends are silent, like three day old death,
Grey like a cold morning makes a fresh breath.
Crashing like waves smashed on rocks by the sea,
Blasted like amber from fossilised trees.

Anita Holbrow

FIGHT OF THE FLAB

This weight hangs on my buxom form
No matter how I try
It hangs in multi-layered folds
And would make a slimmer cry.

One thousand calories a day
They tell me is quite usual
But flab jumps on my hips and thighs
Even with a quick perusal.

I'm quite happy in the winter
When covered from head to foot
In scarves, coats, hats and thermal vest
And my faithful welly boots.

But it's summer that upsets me
When I cower on the beach
With bathing beauties all around
Immaculate and sleek.

It's not so much my pendulous bust
Or my rippling midriff bulge
It's when I remove my clothes at night
I can't see my flipping toes.

But this time I'm going to lose those pounds
No matter what it takes
But first I'll eat that chocolate bar
And I might just tackle that cake.

Jean Hodson-Hirst

THE FOX

I looked out of my window in the dead of night,
And there I saw an amazing sight,
A beautiful fox looking up at me,
With eyes so sharp, and full of curiosity,
And as I watched this beautiful sight,
My heart was filled with pure delight,
He stood so still in the light of the moon,
I prayed he wouldn't disappear too soon,
The wind rustled the leaves on the tree,
He smelt a scent, I prayed it wasn't me,
His glossy coat a-gleaming red,
A huge bushy tail that had no end,
He looked so magnificent in the pale moonlight,
Then quick as a flash . . .
He disappeared into the night!

Erica Gordon

RETIREMENT

Retirement for him isn't good for me,
and it's no good for him this he'll agree.
He's now in my kitchen he's moved this and that
nothing is safe not even the cat.
The shopping is done but no longer by me
we argue a lot and we disagree.
I know I still love him of this he's not sure
but does he still love me as much as before?
With time on his hands no interests as such
what others are doing bothers him much.
Money's a problem where does it go?
We can and do manage but you wouldn't think so.
Our house is for sale like many before
but this one may linger of this I'm quite sure.
If it does sell where will we go?
He wants to go far, but I do not know.

Sandra H Seed

DÉJÀ VU

The endless fear won't go away
Enduring pain from unfelt wrongs
I feel the seams may start to fray
Of patchwork love and pointless songs.

Forbidden words have much to tell
Disclosed in blindness; stab in dark
Transfer of pain, as scent to smell;
Sharp and strong as knife to heart.

Emptiness inspires the mind
The futile memories left behind.
A hollow heart filled with despair,
Encased in fear; life isn't fair.

With truth tattooed upon his arm
I thought I'd be quite safe from harm.
But irony prevails once more,
It's ripped through flesh and pierced the core.

Once again the rain will fall
At least I know that it will cease.
Sometime, when the time will crawl,
The day from which, I'll rest in peace.

Lisa M Harling

SOPHIE

As I watch you sleeping
I almost shed a tear -
I've waited for so long for you
I can't believe you're here.

You really are perfection
From your curls down to your toes -
With big brown eyes and peachy skin
And gorgeous button nose!

I love you more than life itself
My precious baby sweet -
Your cuddles and your happy smiles
Have made my life complete.

Nicky Walker

SINGLE PARENT

Don't give up when you're feeling sad,
A single parent's not that bad,
A lost youth, a lost partner, you do feel cheated,
But that's not enough to be defeated.

Decisions seem endless and money is tight,
Check your benefits and make sure they are right,
Help and support can be got from 'One Plus',
These groups are there for people like us.

Go out with the kids, laugh and have fun,
Life's what you make it, you only get one,
Education, a job, yes do have a go,
At the end of the day it's worthwhile you know.

Single parents are special both mum and a dad,
To their children they help through the good and the bad,
They love and protect the best way they can,
Until their precious offspring become woman or man.

Single parents have courage that is unique,
They can look on the bright side when things look bleak,
The love for their kids is not always spoken,
But the depth of that bond can never be broken.

Sandra Cameron

LOVE IS SO MANY THINGS

There's the love of a man and woman,
And a mother's love for her child,
And the wonderful love in a baby's eyes,
In their first sweet innocent smiles.

There's the love of a child for its parents,
If one joins in their games, or read,
A child indistinctively know it's loved,
Which helps for its future indeed.

There's the love of the beauties of nature,
And the joys that the seasons bring,
- The fairy-like touch of rime-frost,
Or the first lovely flowers of spring.

There's the help of a good Samaritan,
Or support of a friend who cares,
Who has helped us in our darkest hours,
And soothed away our fears.

The devotion of an animal,
Who will stay by one up to the end,
Many a person has cause to bless,
Their faithful four-footed friend.

Sometimes when we're quiet and thinking,
Enjoying a short well-earned rest.
We can think of the love that surrounds us,
And realise how much we are blessed.

E Bowden

COUNTRYSIDE

I do miss the countryside
So green and full of life
Also the flowing river Thane
That ripples through the night.
The birds that start to sing
At the break of dawn
Hedgehogs that creep away to hide
Spiders crawling up our garden walls
And the coming of the eventide.

Oh to have the fresh air smell
The wind blowing lots of gales
How I would feel so well
If I was walking on the dales.
See the beauty all around
Watch the heron taking flight
Autumn leaves falling to the ground
Rabbits running out of sight
As we approach my Meg and I
In the beautiful wonderful countryside.

Eunice Neale

IN THE BEGINNING

The earth was still no wind did blow
A blackness hovered dense and low
No sound was heard in this forsaken place
Then a speck of heaven fell with grace
On to the wild bare earth below
And God looked down and watched it grow
Then dew fell off the speck of green
And formed the oceans that are seen
And God observing earth's new face
Made plans to start the human race
He pondered hard and did concede
The way to meet man's basic need
The mighty oceans soon grew rich
And so appeared the noble fish
On noticing the Lord did frown
There was no melody no sound
Soon the countryside and woods
Resounded with the sound of birds
A gentle wind began to blow
The clouds dispersed the sun did show
Now the Lord was satisfied
He made a vow down deep inside
These were his people down below
And he would love and watch them grow.

Mary Christina McKelvey

FRIENDS

I say to you, my dear friend
Our friendship will never end

We've been there, we've done that
Bought the T-shirt, worn the hat

Shared our first childhood crush
Only to find, we were in a rush

A rush to find our own ways
Amongst the never-ending days

Then together, we stood tall
Through winter, spring, summer and fall

Then at last, for all to see
A transformation, you and me

Now, here we are, all grown up
Love and kindness spilling from the cup

Some tried to put us down
But they never made us frown

As we grew up, getting old
Our precious friendship did unfold

To those around, who we did love
Until one day, from up above

A change in life we did receive
Something so very hard to believe

You breathed your last, that sad day
So goodbye my friend I must say

Of you, my memories are fresh and clear
Kept close and held most very dear

Until one day, when we meet again
No more sorrow, no more pain

Until then, my dear friend
Our friendship will never end.

Rebecca Boardman

THE PRISON WIDOW - 'GOLDFISH BOWL'

To mourn your loss,
  fear the toil ahead.
to live amid,
  though just exist.
an empty soul,
  the pain persists.
to not be free,
  but yet alone . . .
      . . . and know the pain is all your own

To ape a life,
  yet live only in part,
and in so, watch and mark the time
  use change in others as a guide
to invest your hopes in the others' scribe . . .
. . . is a falsehood bearing no proof of action . . .
. . . inviting regret upon reflection.

To raise the child,
  as if from just one source, bring fear of its possible effect.
to feel compelled to compensate
  for one's foolish and initial choice
and to this end; vital years lost
  for the waste brings yet uncounted tears.

Caroline Wyde

TO A CERTAIN PERSON

I am so many years younger than you,
With long blonde hair and eyes of blue.
My skin is firm,my body slim,
No need to waste time in the gym.
Of course I am admired for the way that I talk,
I'm witty and clever and I know how to walk.
I could charm the birds from the trees,
So many men I have brought to their knees.
Why with all this is he with you?
Where did I go wrong? I haven't a clue!

Elaine Naylor

THE HOURS OF THE NIGHT

The sheer delight of a blessed read
'Quality time' - a rare time indeed!
At long last I discover an author whose book
Deserves much more than a flick through look
Depicting the story of village folk, entwining lives and loves
> in tension
Relationships pen-drawn so finely hold firm my full attention
Entwining themes of music, gardening and poetry
With a deep understanding of the seasons - borne so stoically
By earth and village folk alike.
The treasury of books to be found in the bookshop village of hay
Was described, where I too spent a wondrous browsing day.
How I enjoyed that detailed read, I celebrate her writing!
The rural setting, the folk described, her imagery were so to my liking.
How many echoes, chords these words will strike
To countless other readers of authors that they so like
Each to our own choice whether it be romance, adventure
> or biography
Enjoying our reading as part of a shared history
Being all absorbed . . . in an open book.

Ann Brownless

HAPPY BIRTHDAY SHARON

When we learned of your birth
It was the best news on earth
Four long years we had waited for you
We just could not believe
That we had conceived
Our dream of a child had come true

On the day you were born
'Twas a bright Monday morn
Six pounds and eight ounces of love
And the third of July
Will always rate high
As when god sent his gift from above

You grew up from a baby
To a perfect young lady
From school, to work, to a bride
You were never a worry
Just off in a hurry
In our life, you brought nothing but pride

You are there when you're needed
And you're never conceited
You're our daughter, our friend, and our mate
Though you do have one failing
That sends us all reeling
You're not early - you're just a bit late

The last twenty-five years
Passed without tears
You found Peter, and love intertwined
But you still have the time
To keep us in mind
You're so special - just one of a kind.

Love Mum and Dad.

Anne Graham

THE MUSIC OF SPRING

O come Glorious Season, Do Come.
From the song of the blackbird, who
Heralds in spring, and from under his
wings, a mystical season brings.

Like a carpet of ermine, then sweeping
valleys of gold. And let their trumpets
sound for the wonderful creations about
to unfold.

An echo will bound, and bells will ring.
Off valleys and hills, to announce this
most joyous spring.
And a clash of cymbals, and pounds on a
drum, shall all fade away, to the bees'
Gentle hum.

Marian Winsor

DISAPPEARING SEASHORE

Our seashore always used to be
Full of shells and creatures of the sea.
But nowadays all you find
Are stones and rubbish, left by mankind.
As the sea comes in, it always brings
Wood, plastic bags, bottles and tins.
Oh why does our seashore have to be
A graveyard of rubbish for our children to see.
The seashore gradually disappears year after year
Its global warming the scientists fear.
As more and more of our coastline goes
Lots of people are losing their homes
There's not much really that we can do
Other than stop the pollution that's my view
And then the sealife may get a chance to
                                    live and breed
In a nice clean sea full of seaweed.

M A Dale

A Fantasy

I dreamt they sent me on a journey
I asked would it take long?
They said, who knows, perhaps
Three score years and ten
For there are many ways to go
Many paths to choose.

They clothed me in my mortal gown
I asked, what is my task?
They said, to do the will of God.
You have freewill.

I started on the journey
I was enchanted with life -
The will of God forgotten
I pursued a path of pleasure.
Soon I was disillusioned
It did not satisfy a yearning deep within.

On the dusty road of time
I stumbled through a barrier of self
To try a path of duty
It led me to a wilderness of pain.

I thought I would try a path of faith
It was a mighty mountain
But I had made my choice
I could not turn back
I stumbled and fell
Yet reached the peak.

I sank upon my knees
The colour was so beautiful.
They took away the old mortal gown
I was at peace ready and waiting for rebirth.

Irene Henthorne

HIM

He smiled and waved
As I died within;
He didn't realise
My heart had him in.

His innocent smile
Pierced at my soul;
The year without him
Had taken its toll.

I returned the smile
As I held back the tears,
Wondering if I'd love him
For the rest of my years.

Louise Bourne

FAMILY LIFE

From when we're born to the time we marry
No one knows what burdens we'll carry
Teething, crawling, learning to talk
Tumbles we have when learning to walk
School days spent with friend or foe
Nobody knowing how far we'll go
Teenage years, when we start to mature
Learning all about love and allure
Meeting and marrying our partner for life
Bearing children, overcoming strife
Working hard for children and spouse
Seeking promotion, buying a house
When retirement comes around
Peace and tranquillity can be found
Put your feet up, that's the best
Leave the rushing to the rest
Grandchildren come, bringing joy
Be it girl or robust boy
Enjoy it all from start to finish
Before your energy does diminish.

Marion Pollitt

THE CHESTNUT TREE

The sort of thing that amazes me,
Is the birds that live in the chestnut tree.

The birds that live in the chestnut tree,
Belong to the world with you and me.

That sort of thing is so pretty,
But when you hear it is a pity . . .

When all those trees are all chopped down,
There is no trees at all in the town.

So all these birds lose all their homes.
When it's morning they're happy 'cause they use their tones.

Louise Gough (15)

A RETIRING FIRST SCHOOL TEACHER

Dear, dear, Mrs Warburton
So you're retiring from the fray
The time has come to take your ease
No more school every day
Remember the markings and mountings you've done?
Paintings and drawings galore
Remember the reflections you sometimes had
Thinking, 'Tch I wonder what it's all for?'
Well we can say with confidence
That the knowledge you've passed on
Has been of the highest standard
Showing what a great job you've done!
Each year you would get some 'darlings'
It just seemed to be your fate
But then as you got to know them
Things began to fall into shape
The bright ones, the shy, and the naughty
You soon had them all sorted out
Just a look from your book to be quiet
Except for the odd one who still needed a shout
There's been many a mess and a puddle
Enough to cause you frustration
But at the end of the day, when all was tidied away
You felt, *yes,* there was something in *'Education'.*

Mary Wilson

FAMILY

Children, eagerly awaited. A gift from God.
A miracle of fingers, toes, smiles and tears.
The childhood days seem endless to busy parents.
Juggling jobs, home, finances, growing up.
Can I ever be free of washing, homework, cooking, consoling,
Gardening, admonishing, praising?
The need for energy is urgent,
And the pace frenetic - school run,
Ballet, judo, Guides, Scouts, choir practice -
Never a dull moment. Please may I stop?
Too soon the child turns into fractious
Teenager - contrary, outrageous, tearful, sometimes
hateful, but the door is always open, and
That is the bond that binds the family.
As children age and lives
Take many turns bringing joys and
Troubles, the balance shifts. The ebbs and
Flows of fortune pull strongly at the family ties,
And new responsibilities
Come to grown-up children. And parents
Now retired become elder statesmen.

Marjorie Thomson

PRECIOUS MOMENTS

Where did it go, this passage called time,
It goes so quickly, like a very fine wine,
If you're lucky, it is shared, a moment or two,
To be remembered later, by me and you,
Tears of sadness, and those of laughter,
Recalling all, thro' jovial banter,
A lot of ifs, whys, and maybes, better laid to rest,
Even more of did and do's, never to forget,
Precious, tender moments, forged into eternity,
Learning later in life, it's called your destiny,
As time goes by, and the years unfold,
Share these moments, as precious as gold,
Not forgetting, the ones so very dear, that you love,
Gone, but not forgotten, somewhere high up above,
And when grey clouds, hang heavy above your head,
Bring out a little treasure, and smile instead,
Of the one that lifts you, when recovered deep from your heart,
So precious, ne'er forgotten, and ne'er be apart,
Light the candle, see the flickering of its flame,
Raise your glass, to memories, from where they came.

Shirley Atkinson

FRIENDS

Life has many ups and downs
as on its path we tread,
And many people pass our way
as though the years we thread,
Some people come, some people go
but friends they stay forever,
Giving support in times of joy
and help when life is sad,
They are always there with a cheery smile
whether the years are good or bad,
To share our very deepest thoughts
that to no one else we would tell,
To have a friend who is always there
is a joy to touch your heart,
A true good friend, a friend for life
that only death can part.

Rita Webster

DEDICATED TO OUR NAN...

She had the face of an angel.
A heart of gold.
She was loved by all who knew her.
We shall always remember,
The love, that radiated from deep within her.
Her charm, her friendliness.
Her independent, stubborn streak.
The love she had to life, and her family.
This is all that makes her,
The beautiful person we all knew and loved.

The angels took her away,
Away to a place,
Where she will suffer no more pain.
Where she will rest in total peace,
And happiness.
A big piece of our hearts,
Were taken away with nan.
Our loss, was her gain.
She has now peace and contentment.

We can be sure,
She will, always be smiling
Down on us.
The warmth and love,
In our hearts.
Will see us through,
Until we meet again . . .
                        Sleep tight . . .

T Stangroom

ETERNITY

I've lived, I've loved,
I've birthed my child,
I've brought them up,
Which brought my smiles.

I've left my loved one,
All alone,
I've left in my body,
But not in my soul.

I watch over my friends and foe,
But I don't think, they would know,
One day we all will meet again,
From now till then,
I'll gleam and glide,
And watch my husband,
Side by side.

Now I must go,
My husband's come,
To stay by my side,
We've got our home,
A nicer home,
Up on The yonder sky.

We've had our toast,
I know I boast,
For now I rest in peace,

For all I was for many years,
A lonely love struck ghost.

Chris Shepherd

NEVER GIVE UP HOPE

No matter how hard life seems
Never ever give up hope
The soul stores power deep within
Providing us all to cope

So when troubles weigh us down
And we fall into despair
Hold up your head and look around
You'll find the answer somewhere

Problems never last forever
So resist the need to run
Remember that beyond the storm
You'll always find the sun.

S Beeby (15)

MY OWN PLACE . . .

I have a place where I like to go
Let the outside world be fast or slow.
This is my haven, my treasure chest
Where all my troubles are laid to rest.

Here I am soothed of my fears and ills.
Here I am free of the world's treadmill.
I'm in the present, I'm in the past,
Or even into the future cast,

This is my secret, hiding place,
Where I dictate the going pace.
I close my eyes, the world stands still.
I'm who, and what and where I will.

Eileen Monaghan

SUMMER IS A-COMING . . .

Open the doors -
Dust down the table.
Hibernation is over
Now we are able
To enjoy food outside
And that bicycle ride
Over bilberried moors.

Tattooed men in cars
Their arms brown and bare
Rev up their engines,
They haven't a care.
For summer is sizzling
And before it starts drizzling
They'll be in the bars.

For there's sport every day,
Football and cricket.
No place to flee
Before the first wicket,
The stumps and the balls,
The whistles and calls
Are too much, so I pray

For a Pimms on the lawn,
A book and a sunshade;
Rest for the legs,
And then when the tea's made,
The jam and the cake,
And after, I'll take
A nap until dawn!

Angela Stacey

WOMAN TO WOMAN

She knows the signs, she sees her pain
She can guess the problem, she's felt the same
The eyes that glance down when questions are asked
The barriers are put up, the face is masked

She knows the signs, sees the lonely soul
Feels her guilt and sadness that's taken its toll
Only woman to woman can understand
She never meant to betray her man

She knows the signs, it will take time
Realises her despair, it feels much like mine
She's chosen her path, life goes on
She'll only smile again when the ache has gone.

Julie

Touch . . .

If I were deaf
I would still be able to see your smile,
watch you as you wash up and iron,
as you drive the car and mow the lawns,
and feel your arms around me,
as I always do.
If I were blind
I would still hear your laugh;
the sounds you make as you sit on the bed
getting dressed; your derisory shouts at the TV
when you disagree with what's being said;
your unprintable comments on newspaper articles;
and little would be lost while you describe the dreams we share,
the hopes we both dare to wish for . . .
And with your hand in mine, close as always,
I could feel my way in the dark,
as I always do.
And if I were both blind and deaf,
you would still lie beside me in our bed,
caressing the contours of my body,
touching my mind,
and feeling my innermost thoughts,
as I feel yours.
Our love would be as it has always been,
a source of healing;
and in the darkness of the midnight hour,
in the silence of the sleepless summer night,
just your touch would be the only sense I need
to heighten the feeling of love.
As it always does.

J Margaret Service

TRUTH

In my youth -
I ate truth for breakfast
and daydreams for lunch.
I thought I could save the world,
and feed the starving millions.
I imagined prejudice would disappear
and I could change things for the better.

Now I am older -
I lunch on broken promises and
                shattered illusions.
I do not eat breakfast at all -
because truth has become
         too bitter to swallow.

Brenda Heale

WEDDING GUEST

A Wedding invitation so I must have something new
An outfit no-one's seen me in, and nothing else will do
But it's time to be responsible, time to be mature
I'm going to wear something that I know I've worn before

And so I form my strategy with military precision
And no-one else believes this quite unnatural decision
I must establish my objectives, an outfit's to be planned
My drawers are full to bursting, and my wardrobes are all jammed

That cropped top with those trousers? No it makes my arse look huge
I don't want to wear a jacket as a bit of subterfuge
They pinch a bit, and they don't fit, that skirt and top are dated
That skirt's too tight, that looks a sight and that suit is overrated

I've tried all the permutations - and now I'm in despair
I'm going to this wedding and I've not a thing to wear!
A friend comes to the rescue with a dress and matching hat
But now there's just a week to go and I won't be seen dead in that!

So I bought last season's flowery frock at half price in the sale
And a trendy little cardi in a lighter shade, quite pale
There's just one day to go, I've seen some sandals that are nice
I think I'll go and get them, they're at a discount price

Some might call me shallow, but I don't give a damn
I work bloody hard all week, and spend because I can!
I love to shop, don't want to stop, it's the reason we exist
You can't resist a bargain when it's there and can't be missed

Some get high on Heroin, think Ecstasy's their thrill
But I hit my Nirvana with the ringing of that till.

Nikki Roche

TIRED AGAIN

I really am tired and so bloody stressed
I can't even be bothered to get myself dressed
I want to go out, I'm too sodding scared
I'm alone in my home, with no one that cared
I ironed today, yet only a few
None were my things, they all belong to you
I'm feeling so sick I don't want to eat
Yet all I can think of are roasties and meat
My husband comes home, but I won't cheer up
He brought me some milk but in the wrong cup
So I started shouting and he got upset
I don't want a cuddle you're covered in sweat
I hate feeling tired I feel such a pain
But they're all so used to it
              'She's at it again'.

Kirsty Charnell

A POEM ABOUT MEN

Many men can't cook or clean
Or even use a washing machine
Beer and sex is all they crave
Leading them to an early grave
All they do is watch the telly
Dribbling onto their beer belly!
A man is good in one small leisure
That is if you want some pleasure!

Lisa Massarella (16)

HOUSEWIFE

A housewife works extremely hard,
no one notices of what she imparts.
Praises are few and far apart -
her work horrendous from the very start.
But calmly, impassively, she leads the way -
for hers is to do and always obey.
Neither objects or agrees to most -
ambiguous being, a wonderful host.
Her children she struggles to bring up at best,
She considers them all as good as the rest.
At heart, she is kind, thoughtful and just -
Caring is a characteristic - a real must.
A wife is not always as easy as one must agree . . .
To keep to the vows: 'honour, love and obey',
compromise and caring are almost the key.
When the other half asks her to make the tea?
She answers politely and carries on regardlessly.

Teresa Wood

SOFT TOP

I am the girl
in the red
drop-head sports car.

I make your mouth water.
I wear sunglasses
and my long hair blows in the wind.

I am the girl
you want to get your hands on,
the one you'd know what to do with.

I am the girl
in the shiny red lipstick,
you know what I could do with, too.

I am the girl
in the only car you don't mind
overtaking you: 'Cop a load of that!'

I am the girl your girlfriend hates.
I am the rich-bitch, man-stealing
cow with a convertible,

and yes, basically,
I want to get
right up your nose.

I want a bumper
sticker that says
'Eat dirt turkeys.'

(I'm quite nice actually, somebody's Mrs.)
I'm your fantasy
urban myth.

Vali Stanley

OREA

This love we hold
This love we share
This heart we hurt
For those who dare
This myriad, this rainbow lost
Is carved so deep
Though to our cost

Love hath no price
No sale tag given
It comes as clouds
Upon us driven
With gust and fury
Like no other

This love.

Christine H Graveson

THE ENIGMA

In the depths of those eyes
I see torment and trial.
Into two pools of black
I stare and ask 'Why?'
I ask myself 'What?' and
'How where and when?'
I think up an answer
Then must think again.
A mystery, enigma,
A puzzle, a trick.
I gaze in those eyes and
Ask 'What makes him tick?'

Rosemary Hadley

ONLY SIXTY MINUTES?

From smouldering, we flared, flamed
Our fiery burning, blazing could scorch to touch
I fell for my infernal Dante.
Now shrouded in ashes, charred remains,
Still smoking, fuming;
Branded by the flames of love turned hate.

Once diamond-hard and crystal-sharp
Yields devastatingly to your wrecking ball
The cracks were riven; driven through by your anger
Each knife-edged shard you'd wield
The final strike and I lay shattered
Broken so expertly; the cold wind of your
Departure scatters my fragile pieces.

I'm still biting brutal, brittle needles
Shrapnel scars rake my emotions to shreds
Defences beaten down and gnawed
Sacrificed on a rusting, bloodied stake.

And even as the shadows fall, obscure the
Boundary of my limits,
I strive to understand,
And know that this, my darkest hour,
Is only sixty minutes.
I strive to stand.

Helen Houghton

To Lose A Father

The time I thought would never
  Come is happening today,
Heaven needed another angel
  So God's taken you away.
I want to thank you Dad for
  Everything you've done
I'll look back on our yesteryears
  And think of joy and fun
You've been an inspiration,
  You've taught me everything I know,
But now I know the time is
  Here and you have had to go.
I don't know who I'll turn to
  Now with problems I need to share,
I've always taken it for granted
  That you were always there.
Please Dad give me strength
  To carry on my life
And help me to look after
  Your best pal who is my mum,
                        - your wife.

Ruth Mellor

ANSWER MY PRAYER

I dare not think of tomorrow
It fills me with so much sorrow.
The world we live in is not a happy place,
There's nothing human left in the human race.
Death and destruction, famine and war
Fighting and killing and unholy law.

No peace and tranquillity,
We've lost the ability
To live side by side with each other
respecting no matter what colour or creed
Our fellow man as our brother.

Somewhere at sometime, we'll probably need
An out-stretched hand friendly and warm
We won't notice the colour, black or white
The friendship it offers feels so right.
To know that there's care
Would answer my prayer.

Lydia Rose Collins

TRANQUILLITY

Peacefully passing
Time never asking
Slowly requiring no
Reason at all

Timefully telling
Easily quelling
Riotous noise
From everyday life

Listening and letting
Sun always setting
Silently accepting
The end of the day.

Su Perry

MY BATHROOM MIRROR

I love my bathroom mirror,
It does great things for me.
My skin looks smooth and fresh,
Just like it ought to be.

I have a healthy colour,
My cheeks have quite a glow.
I look so much younger there,
If only it were so!

Not like my other mirrors,
They're really most unkind
They can't be right - I look a sight,
My skin's so old and lined.

They make me feel unhappy,
And leave me quite depressed.
Not like my bathroom mirror,
Which shows me at my best.

I love my bathroom mirror,
It's very plain to see.
The reason why I like it so
It's very kind to me!

Phyllis Hall

THE ELDEST SISTER

I hated being the eldest of three
having two sisters look up to me

If I faltered, if I fell
they were always there to run and tell

Parents shouting 'They're watching you'
you need to behave, show what to do

The pressure of maturing was too intense
my small pool of knowledge was supposed to be immense

I craved to be older, so I could be me
instead of a number, one of three

I fled the nest to a bedsit alone
solitude, peace, no sisters to moan

Even then I was expected to be
the big sister who still visited for tea

Now they've got children, families of their own
they still ask advice, by visit or phone

I've reached the grand age of thirty-three
but still I'm the sister they each want to be.

Janice Wilson

A PRIVATE FEAR

I can face a rainy day
When the car has broken down
And I'm never that put out
When someone jumps the queue.
I don't mind being up all night
When the baby's being sick
And it doesn't bother me at all
If I run out of milk.
I'm not the least concerned
If I burn the Sunday roast
And I really do not care
If my home is rather shabby.
I would be the last to moan
If the postmen went on strike
And I wouldn't turn a hair
If a comet crashed to earth.
But there is one thing that makes me sweat
And suffer sleepless nights,
I shudder at the very thought
That it should happen again.
My private fear, my private dread
I cannot bear the thought
That I should wander down the road
With my skirt tucked in my pants!

Jane Nutting

VISIONS LOST

She looked up from her iron

'Tom, Tom. There's a rhinoceros
charging across the sky. Look.'
'Dinnae be sae fanciful, woman.
It's only a dirty big cloud.'
She bowed her head to the Tuesday chore
pitying the poor man who once saw
fairies in the fire but now could see
no further than the daily news.

Next time she glanced through the window
someone had colour-washed the sky
and begun to paint storm clouds.
Heavy black bled into charcoal,
charcoal into clerical grey,
clerical grey into drab putty.
Here and there blobs of cotton wool
dabbed at the peeps of celestial blue.

A fire-breathing dragon drifted by
to be dispersed in its own wisps of smoke.
A proud bald eagle, outlined in
shining shimmer, perched with wings
outstretched like a guardian angel
to ward off the approaching storm.
To no avail. Lightning knifed
through the gloom, thunder cannoned.

The rain fell in curtains of living water,
obscuring her visions.

Betty Harcombe

BEING HARASSED

Our neighbours
Living on my doorstep
Inviting themselves in
With choking voices
And Victorian cemetery tombstone teeth
Waiting for me to come home
Like an eagle for its prey
Smoking Embassy No 6
When they say they only have one lung
(Between them probably)

Amanda Hockley

BODIES . . .

. . . like oceans
with hidden depths to explore,
for peril or pleasure.
Crevices and hollows
seek investigation
as the slow fish
awakens to soft ripples on its flesh.
Dark forest fronds
glisten with dewy expectation
fingering the surface,
for air.
Then skyward
and seaward
champagne send-off,
emptied and contained,
filled and fulfilled
two bodies
all at sea.

Sue Hansard

MOM'S TOP TIPS ON HOW TO KEEP YOUR MAN

Now don't forget when you are wed,
to keep your husband properly fed.

Clean the house and keep it neat,
and warm the slippers for his feet.

See the children quietly play,
you know he's been at work all day.

Cut down on bills, sew and knit,
'cause if you don't he'll have a fit.

A home in total harmony
to where he can return,
no matter how it is achieved
his wife must quickly learn.

For if you don't,
and he's upset,
He's down the pub
you can bet.

Well, it must have been too perfect.
He needed more it seemed.
A woman in total contrast,
with whom he lied and schemed.

If my daughter marries,
into which she may feel pressed.
I'll tell her not to take advice.
But wing it like the rest.

Susan Rowley

UNTITLED

She's a little old lady, we all tower above her
But no one can doubt we think the world of her.
I remember the time her life was so hard.
Six of us squabbling, outside toilet, a yard.
A purse often empty she had plenty to give
She taught us true values to love and to live
To care for each other, the weak and the old
And there's more to this life than treasures like gold.
She's one in a million, a cut above the rest.
To me she's my mam. She's simply the best.

Adrienne Bell

I AM YOUR OWN

What can I say to you
you who gave your all.
What can I do for you,
I really feel so small.
Words will not come
and yet I know
you know my heart
and love me so.
You hear each sigh.
You hear each groan.
You know my needs.
I am your own.

Sheila Whipp

THE OMAGH BOMB . . . REMEMBERING

Why? The grief. The pain.
A blow to the heart;
Tears shed again.
Why? Are we made to suffer
the loss of a mother, child
what condolence can we proffer?

Men and women. Young and old
For what inhuman cause
Have these lives been sold?
Why? I fail to understand
How bombers hold life
less dear than land.

Take time to stop: reflect and pray.
Scarred with wounds and hurts
Will tainted dreams fade away?
Death and terror. Violence. Hate.
A better future in sight?
How long must we wait?

A moment of silence.
A gesture of peace.
Why all this violence
From the bombers - the beasts.
United in horror. Together we quail
Alone now and waiting,
Hoping love will prevail.

Tracey McClelland

56

A POEM FROM MY HEART:

Trapped . . .

A reflection from a window pane, staring back at me,
it looks so trapped inside that frame, yet I am standing free.
Or is it I am the reflection and the world is one big frame,
trapped inside this world for life just like the window pane.

Vicki Michele Loveday

GUESS WHO?

All loving
All enduring
All forgiving
All caring,
      Guess who? . . . (Mother Theresa - Calcutta)

All strong hold with an arm
All who could do no harm
Ruled with an iron arm
All famous all around,
      Guess who? . . . (Maggie Thatcher)

All sexy
All rexy
All flirty
All swing - ky,
      Guess who? . . . (Monica)

All Purity
All Dignity
Born Immaculate
Rise Immaculate,
      Guess who? . . . (Virgin Mary)

All attractive
All manipulative
All dazzling
All sparkling,
      Guess who? . . . (Marlyn M)

All exploiting
All commanding
All collecting shoes
All ambitious,
      Guess who? . . . (Imelda Marcos)

All loveable
All admirable
Win many hearts
Die Queen of hearts,
   Guess who? . . . (Diana Princess)

All writing
All investigating
Solve the murder
All with the hammer,
   Guess who? . . . (Angela L)

J B Henderson

GETTING OLDER

I'm getting older day by day
And starting to feel the pinch,
My waistline gives the game away
Growing inch by inch.

I must not grumble, must not groan
When I feel an ache or twinge,
It's nature's way of telling me
To slow down and not whinge.

To be an 'oldie' has its perks,
Not many it is true,
I get a bus pass, oh! what joy,
But I still have to queue.

I can stay in bed quite late
Or stay up late at night,
Without my parents telling me
To do my homework - right.

I have a dog who keeps me young
And keeps me on my toes,
We go for long walks every day,
Stops me thinking of my woes.

But life is sweet as I can tell,
To be an oldie is quite good,
I hope to live for long years yet
By eating healthy food.

And so as time goes rolling by
We cannot stop the years,
So keep on smiling, do your best
And do not shed those tears.

Marian Smith

LIFE

If life sometimes gets you down,
Take a stroll and look around.
It will make the day seem brighter,
The pressures will become much lighter.

When life you cannot bare,
Think there's always someone there.
No-one should ever be so dull,
Live life to the very full.

If life should cause a frown,
Lift yourself up off the ground.
Click the heels of your shoes,
Laugh and throw away the blues.

Live life with a lot of care,
Even when you might not dare.
Every morning should give you a lift,
Life is a very priceless gift.

Gillian A Fitzpatrick

Rain

What do you think of the falling rain,
Do you say, 'Oh heck it's raining again,'
Do you ever think of the goodness in it,
As it opens a bud almost every minute.
As it waters the flowers and brings forth the corn
And water is used when a child is born.
It has so many uses we are apt to forget,
that we shouldn't get angry each time we get wet.
What would we do without the rain,
We'd suffer from famine again and again.
Like far off lands who suffer from drought,
They would wonder what we were shouting about.
How they would love to see falling rain,
And be free from hunger sickness and pain.
So next time it's raining and we're tempted to moan,
Just turn again to *him* on the throne,
And say thank you Lord for the rain that *You* give,
Please give it to others that they also may live.

Elizabeth Boyle

TEARS OF LIGHT

Smoke, death, carnage, violence and fears
The innocent victims who will wipe their tears?
The dead who have gone and can feel no more pain,
Now rest peacefully with Jesus for their deaths were not in vain.
The little angels the Blessed Virgin has taken in her arms
She has wrapped them in her mantle safely away from harm.
This country that we live in is like an oozing sore
But can it only be treated forever, ever more?
Like a terminal disease that there is no cure,
It has its good and bad days of that you can be sure.
Two traditions like a cancerous tumour feeds,
Upon this land that needs to sow new seeds.
Let us sever these two growths that do not give good fruit,
And produce one healthy sprout that all will suit.
For in this town of Omagh where two rivers symbolically run,
Let a new dawn arise with a bright shining sun.
To bind these two communities into a knot so strong.
Enabling them to shoulder this awful terrible wrong.
And in the darkness of their anguish may there emerge a voice of light,
Bringing hope, strength and inspiration for a future that will be bright.

Veronica Harley

An Autobiographical View

When I was a child,
I wanted to be wild.
But I was confined
In *their* world.

When I was a wife,
I thought 'This is life,'
But I was confined
In *his* world.

When I was a mother,
I thought nothing other,
But I was confined
In *their* world.

I want to be free,
To be only me,
I want to be confined
In *my* world.

Susan Rushby

IF YOU ONLY KNEW

If my illness was physical,
Then my recovery would be a miracle,
But it's not, it's mental,
So it's important to be gentle.

The harsh words that you spoke so freely,
Words that you meant so sincerely,
Words that left me in despair,
Words that told me that you didn't really care.

My tears flowed like a river, of grief,
Tears that you ignored to make the conversation brief,
Did I really deserve the pain that you caused,
Maybe it's a message which needed to be reinforced.

A message that tells me that you are suffering too,
because it's so out of character and it's not like you,
Being brutally honest isn't always the best way,
Not when the consequences are hard ones to pay.

You may have your own problems that you needed to share,
If that's so, don't shut me out because I really do care,
Since I last spoke to you my mind's in a turmoil,
Because I've always thought our friendship to be one so loyal.

Hassling you just isn't my style,
So I am prepared to wait, should it take a while,
I appreciate the busy lifestyle that you lead,
I admire you because you're always in need.

Thank you for taking the time to read this poem,
Even though it's left me totally open,
I can promise you good times ahead,
But only if you feel our friendship isn't dead.

Jane Taylor

SAD DAYS

Days drag on and tears keep falling,
  Nights are long and days keep dawning,
All my dreams are slowly drifting,
  He opens his eyes and my heart keeps lifting.

Tons of memories come flooding back
  But words to say I seem to lack,
We danced, we laughed, we said goodbye,
  And now it's tears and many sighs.

Happy memories fill my heart,
  Very sad we had to part,
All I wish for you my dear,
  Is sweet dreams and no more tears.

Mari Gilmore

BIRTH . . .

To feel the warmth on my body
Deep eyes shining within my sight
From pain to emotion
did lighten up my life
You came with a sparkle
and a warmth which lighted within
Those first new found
moments are never forgotten.

Vanessa P Cartwright

FIRST VISIT TO THE CHIROPODIST

She strutted in, emitting
An aura of command.
A jerky piece of person
At home with sergeants' stripes.
Feeling apprehensive, seated as
Instructed,
Feet totally at her mercy
For the order of the day.
She seemed to know her stuff
Advice was quickly given
In short staccato phrases.
A rub a dub here
A shaving there
A cream applied
And then dismissed
To make a place
For the next one in the
Waiting game.

Jean Thompson

I BELIEVE

I believe in little leprechauns
And fairy rings upon the lawn
I believe a fiery dragon stands
Beside the mystic from a magic land

I believe that beauty in a spell did sleep
Until the prince to her side did creep
He kissed her once before he told her
Within his love he would enfold her

I believe love comes to those who wait
And love is its own reward
I believe for those who truly love
Their love is a mighty sword

I believe to my side my prince will fly
And take me to that magic kingdom there on high
We will live among the leprechauns and
Dance in fairy rings upon the lawn.

Dawn Johnson

UNTITLED

The life of the beauty
Prolonged hands caressing human flesh
Her eyes closed obscuring the outside
She is captured
He hides his face
It is buried in the warmth of her hair
The colour of flesh is moulded
Into one . . . forever.
How can one portray such a painting?
Expressionism lives!

Christine Mullin

ANOTHER DRENCHING

My friend arrived once more, in tears
this was the third time in one week
and to hear her speak, one could see
she was yet another victim;
another victim of his chauvinism
another victim of his disrespect of womanhood
another victim, whom would cut off his . . .
if only she could.

What could I say?
I had been there so many times
taking the gibes, flinching at pinches
arriving at my friend's home once more
in tears.

Men . . . with their superior bites
and smug delights in causing stress
on top of that which nature dishes out
every month.
We bleed, we wrestle with PMT
we cope
or do we?

How many more women have to break in two
before some kind of law passes through?
How many will feel suicidal
before personnel decides to listen?
How many will someday be in the position
to do the same to those whom deny
with every lie
so plausible?

Harassment . . . drenched embarrassment
biting the core of nature's sodden fruit.

Elizabeth Wilson

THE LONE NIGHTWALKER

Long dark days of winter's rain and mist
Give way without a battle; to even lower temperature
Facing the cold, when the garden looks night bare
With just the twinkle of little snowdrops
Showing spring will not take long

My mind is trapped and bound as I visualise the worst
In the greyness of the wasteland where loneliness prevails
Along the hedgerow of a field, a barn owl
Catches my gaze; and plucks a quick mouse
Silently showing off, soft downy feathers

In a flash, it passes its catch from claw to beak
Pausing nearby skilfully on rotting timber
To swallow, then back into secluded retreat
The lone nightwalker looks on in the freeze
And shudders with dread as a rat scampers freely

A feeling of tension abounds in the air
As magic, the rhythm of snow has begun
This passion love hate drama that flows
To the beat and the dance of life
Respite found, it seemed

For a moment, one senses the gloom is lifted
Shining trinkets of night touched not a tear
Time to stop and enjoy the new white
Or where my dream could be right now
A lover of nature, and sweet warmth
                                    of day.

Machiella Reid

MY VILLAGE

My youth was spent in the countryside,
With trees and fields and spaces wide.
With animals upon the farm,
And cottages so snug and warm.
Summer smells of new-mown hay
Autumn leaves a bright array,
Winter snow is drifting deep,
In spring the bleating of the sheep,
The humming of the busy bees,
The summers cooled with gentle breeze
The dragonflies with pretty wing
Above the pond is hovering.
So let us save our countryside,
With trees and fields and spaces wide,
And let our children see the farm
And live in cottages snug and warm.

D E Tully

CARLA MY DAUGHTER

The tiny life wasn't mine to keep,
happy memories are kept, hidden so deep,
Dare not to mention the beautiful name,
of the daughter that brought me shame,
The decisions are made, though they're not mine,
get the baby adopted, she'll forget in time,
Carla my beautiful, precious baby,
given to others so a family there'd be,
The days, the months, the years roll by,
my tears and feelings I have to hide,
My search has started, O I hope I find,
the little girl that once was mine,
Explain to her, I hope I can
All I ever wanted was to be her mam.
(all my love Carla always)

Maxine Spencer

PASSION

Am I alone feeling this
hurt,
this pain, this anguish
that reaches inside and pulls tears
from every part of me -
that tears every part of me,
leaving me wounded and gasping?

You look puzzled.
Do you really not understand?
Or do you pity me,
this defeated wreck of a woman
beaten down by her own hand?

Am I alone feeling this
love,
this eagerness, this yearning
that moves inside and finds no catch -
but catches joy in every part of me,
collecting me whole and hopeful?

Don't hold back.
Hold my hands and share with me
your hurt, your pain, your love, your joy.
Together we can heal each other.
Together
neither of us is
alone.

Janet Eldred

PLAYING THE GAME

When games we used to play no longer please
They ought to change.
No tossing coins
We need to re-arrange.
Participating couples have to choose;
Unless each stands to win
They both will lose.
If some can 'play the game' then why not all?
There's lots of sense in learning to 'play ball'.

When we played 'catch' you seemed so strong
We prayed we might be caught
'Higher and higher'
You whirled us from the ground
The quarry sort.

You never did like 'playing house'
We should have known
That you'd go off and leave us
On our own
We didn't walk together as we planned
Your game was 'following my leader'
We understand.

So we play 'snap'.
We snap at you
And you will hit hard back
Then games of skill
The one who holds most tricks
Can win the pack.

And should we play 'I spy'
To put an end
To games of love
No more than 'let's pretend',
Reflecting upon partners who deceive
And offer not true love, but 'make believe'.

Why not accept that lots of us are weak
Far better that we run away to 'hide'
And never 'seek'.

Pamann

THE QUESTION

I was just going to speak to you
When you walked out the door:
The words were just coming, I was almost ready
To ask you a question,
Almost ready to hear your reply
When you walked out the door
And you closed it behind you.

So many years of trying to speak,
Fumbling for words that could not reach you,
Groping, grasping, grappling against time . . .

Perhaps it would have been The Question:
Perhaps it would have been The Answer
That I have so often tried to imagine,
So often tried to pull out of the hat
Like the last of a thousand raffle tickets;
So often tried to pull out of my brain
That was never quite ready to find me the clue
Of how to speak to you.

Now you have closed the door.
I watched you go . . .

Will it always be so,
The last tiny piece of porcelain missing from the broken cup,
The tiny lost piece that would have made it whole
Again? Or for the first time?

Oh more lost than a piece of porcelain is
The question . . . *The* Question:
And beyond the furthest reach of imagining
The answer - *The* Answer -
That might have made me whole.

Jenny Desoutter

LONELY HEARTS CLUB

Bargain price rejects,
We're giving away,
Hearts and souls,
Every day.

Bargain price rejects,
Three for a pound,
Make a date and
Hope he comes round.

Bargains galore,
Come into our store,
If you don't like the first
We've always got more.

So don't sit at home,
All lonely and blue,
We've bargain price rejects
Just for you!

Camilla Jane

DAYLIGHT FADING
(For Jane)

I stand waiting
at the day's edge
searching for something
but not quite knowing what
a memory maybe
or a feeling
hidden deep within
the darkest corners of my mind
I look into the dimming light
and frail skeletal figures
walk silently past me
their faces tinged with death
and then out of the fading daylight
she comes toward me
so much confidence she has given me
she sparked the fire that
now burns so brightly inside me
but then just as quickly as she came
she is gone.

Kimberley Mather (16)

LOVER

I waited by the edge of the hungry sea.
For the man I believed I would marry one day
But once again, you weren't there for me,
And time, like the sea, ebbed away.

Lover, I never meant to be
Another morsel for the sea.

I rested on the shifting sand
I prayed you would be true
To the ring you placed upon my hand
And my love for only you.

Lover I never meant to be
Intimate with eternity.

Susan Turbitt

TO A FRIEND

Jane,
Today in your eyes I see pain.
Who has wounded you?
Will you not share
The burden you bear
With those who care for you?

Sylvia M Malt

ODE TO A PSYCHIATRIST

Psychiatrists en masse are an individual breed
Trained to study complex minds in need
Probing to find how the brain operates
In patients willing to co-operate.
Drugs are administered to obviate
Deranged minds so to alleviate
Tension, stress, anxiety, depression
All syndromes of life's recession.
Varied causes can be discovered
Through psychoanalysis will be recovered
To normal thinking and adjustment
To cope with life's problems and re-adjustments.

Avril Buckley

What a Good Bloke

What a good bloke,
He'd do anything for you,
Yes, but what about us,
Move stuff, run fro and to,
For you and you and you.

Not for us such a good bloke,
Jobs need doing,
Mend that wear and tear,
Spend time and effort at home,
No, much better to help elsewhere.

Ann Thomason

EGG

Into your cupped dry palm I dropped
the smooth cool curve of an egg.
Its shell strong as the transparency of bone
behind eyes,
cradling the slick curd of brain.

Thin as the skin of the frosted world in a blue space.

The curve of a face,
the arc of a cool tower,
an aeroplane slingshot to heaven.
The blue horizon.

The rind of the lonely moon.

Within, a vitreous slop.
Thin wet rounds turned to thick juice;
poured out, not left to set -
harden as clay -
and unpick the white cathedral membrane from inside.

Pat Saunders

THE DAY AND THE LIFE

The Golden Goddess rose
Before all the slaves to the light.
Falling from where?
- The beautiful void.
Caressing concupiscent beings,
Flooding dry canyons of Muse,
Yet draining from those who don't care.

Old deafening darkness descends
Howling his tales of the night
Dwelling in Lunar lair,
Through whispering noise,
Shall tease susceptible beings
To comprehend imperceptible cues.
We excite in nescient fear; to embrace few shall dare.

Roisin Keys

TO A LOVED ONE

I loved you so much, more than you'll ever know,
I loved you with all my heart,
Shot with Cupid's arrow right from the start
Oh, yes I loved you so.

When at a distance you came into view
My heart flipped over, I was sure you knew -
My heart beat so fast when you were near,
I was sure you would hear it, my dearest dear
Oh, yes I loved you so.

I never intended to succumb to your charms,
But as a man to love you were my choice,
I fell in love with your lovely voice,
How I longed to be held in your arms.

Oh, how I loved you, so handsome and tall,
A man of many talents, oh so gifted,
When thinking of you dear my spirits were lifted,
A good kind man most respected by all.
I hoped to make you happy, I did my best,
But you thought I was a bit of a pest.

I must have loved You?
I wished and prayed you would love me some day,
Didn't want us ever to have to part
Such a pity that it turned out you were gay
I had loved you in vain - such a pain in my heart.

I made up my mind to love you no more,
But then I said I would still be your friend,
Didn't want my dreams ever to end,
In my thoughts I see you there at your door
Oh, how I loved you, - I love you still,
My dear friend, I always will.

Rosanna Lee

MOTHERS

They should hold your hand, wipe your nose
Wash and iron all your clothes.
Laugh and skip about with you, clap their
hands to peek-a-boo!

Walk around the park with you,
Play One two buckle my shoe.
Stick your pictures to the wall.
Hug and kiss you when you fall.

Read you stories all night long,
Know the words of your favourite song.
Kiss you goodnight, hear your prayers.
Then quietly creep down the stairs.

They sometimes laugh, sometimes cry.
The hardest part of all is when mothers say
Goodbye . . .

Ann Hicks

WHY?

Why, when I'm all tarted up for a date
Do I ladder my one pair of tights?
Why, in strange pubs, when I go to the loo
Can I not find a switch for the light?
Why, when I rush out because I am late
Do I find that I haven't a key?
I've looked for an answer, but not found one yet.
Oh, why does it happen to me?
Why, when I get rid of one nasty spot
On my chin, does another appear?
Why, when I'm feeling in romantic mood
Would he rather go out for a beer?
Why, when we've left all the stops far behind
Do the kids need to stop for a wee?
I've looked for an answer, but not found one yet
Oh, why does it happen to me?
Why, when I'm starving to lose half a stone
Does my bum look as big as before?
Why, with three bags full of shopping to hold
Is there no one to open the door?
Why, when I'm needing a sherry (or two)
Does my friend call, who only drinks tea?
I've looked for an answer, but not found one yet
Oh, why does it happen to me?

Pat Witlea

AFTER THE SURGEON'S KNIFE

Our fingers curl with loving
familiarity - and we touch.
You entice me deep into you,
I am desperate to be with you,
Where we fall inside each other
Sacred world where we are one.

We move together speaking
our own language - without words.
Reach within me I am scared that,
I can now no longer hear you,
Locked outside our private Eden,
Now my womanhood has gone.

You coax my senses sharper
gently telling me - I am whole.
Your love calls through empty spaces,
I can feel the thunder spreading,
Spring to life each place within me,
I am woman - coming home.

Helen Mary Miller

MY SON IAN

I walk along the seashore
Gazing out to sea
I look up to the sky
Why O Lord
Did you take my son
From me.

I climb the steps
To the prom above
The wind and rain
In my face
I turn and look
For your little dog
There she is
Sheltering by my legs
Your dog and I
We sit alone
Both knowing deep down
You can't come home.

Barbara Parker

THANK GOD MY PREGNANCY IS ALMOST OVER

I know I've been distant and seemed in distress
It's just that I feel my life's such a mess
I won't make excuses for feeling this way
But everything's new I don't want to be gay
I can't wear my clothes I feel oh so fat
I want to be slim no answer to that
My life is now changing and all for a child
I'm feeling so dull, I used to feel wild
I just want a shoulder on which I can cry
No shoulder seems comfy, I don't know why
So all my emotions are locked in my heart
I don't want to be lonely, but I want to be apart
And if I seem different, you won't understand
Just please grit your teeth and hold out your hand.

Kirsty Charnell

LOST YOUTH

When I was young and in my prime,
He called me 'honey' all the time.
My hair, he said, was like spun silk,
Complexion just like creamy milk.
My eyes were of a lovely hue,
A shade he thought like cornflower blue.
My smile was warm, my arms inviting,
My body slim and so exciting.
Into his life I brought great joy,
He swore he was a lucky boy.

Well, that was 40 years ago,
And now I'm someone I don't know.
My hair is grey, my eyes are dim,
I've aches and pains in every limb.
My cheeks have lost their rosy glow,
My repartee and wit are slow.
We've no more secrets, no more chat,
His sweet talk now is for the cat.
No more the centre of his life,
He'll introduce me as 'the wife'.

Margaret Waite

DREAMS

I want to walk with you, and talk with you
To eat, and drink with you; and be with you
I want to work and play with you, start each day with you
To share comforting silences, and friendly noises with you

I want to joke with you, and argue with you
To sleep, and dream with you; to caress and fondle you
To travel and stay home with you; develop and grow with you

I need to make love with you, in every single way with you
To laugh, cry, live and die; to end each day with you
To share what I am with you; to know that 'we' matter with you
To release passion, desire, to fly higher and higher with you

This is a dream, an unobtainable dream
For you are but a whisper, partly heard in a never-ending wind.

Sandy Ingram

THE FEELING OF LAZY SUMMER

Palm fronds wave in the barely discernible movement of air,
While a pink haze hangs soft on the darkening horizon.
Sweet smells, almost indescribable, but totally memorable, linger,
All adding to the faint memories of the day passing.
Flesh celebrating the hot glow of the kiss of the sun.
I try to remember something intangible - just out of reach.
Into my head floods the feeling of lazy summer and the decadent
flavour of ease.

Rosemary Hicks

MOON

Galleon moon slips down her gangway
Spilling sprayed champagne
To tempt the stars, to glitter their eyes
In disordered profusion.
Elasticate their beams to dreaming,
Swivelling descent, gliding, uncertainly
Down.

It is she who hypnotises the atmosphere,
Stares placidly through solid darkness,
Then chops her gaze from leaf
To stem, to branch,
To roots,
To . . .
. . . a furry tail dart, sweep, then
Vanish.

It is she who takes her broom
And gathers life, movement and sleep
In her quilted purse, safe and soft.

Drowsing wearily, she presses her orchid children
Beside her, and rests.
But, a flame-glow enriches her eye
With desire to sail,
Expand her shores, heaving.

So, her craft rocks, and is tossed,
And her woolly, deep murmur
Of protection plunges
The dawn anchor
To weigh her under.

Ann Zastawecki

SHIPS THAT PASS IN THE NIGHT

The butterfly on the flower,
and moving on

The sunshine on the sea
and gone

The raindrop in the shower
lost within the hour

The mist upon the mountain
dissolved within the fountain

The lovers meeting once at night
will they meet again?

. . . they might.

Helen Howe

FRAGMENTS

The huge lunch party was over.
The people were well fed. They turned to go home, satisfied.
Satisfied, not only from hunger, but by the fact that they had just
witnessed a miracle.

What a day!
What a story!
What a lot to talk about as they rose to leave.

As they left, only the fragments remained.
And the disciples.
And Jesus.
'Pick them up' He commanded.
'But, Lord, it's late . . . we're tired already'
'Pick them up.'
'But, Lord, what use are they anyway?'

What use? Twelve baskets of food could go a long way.
Perhaps home with each disciple.
Perhaps as a love-gift to the most needy among the crowd.
Perhaps just left to feed the birds.
But they represented another miracle, missed by so many of
the original 5000.
Those baskets represented what God could do, could still do,
even after most people thought there was nothing more to be done.

God, the God of fragments.
The One who delights to take the bits, the left-overs, the scrag-ends,
And bless them.
All that His disciples need do is to see them, recognise them,
and pick them up.

Let nothing be wasted, least of all the broken pieces.

Heather Henry

COPING

Yesterday it would have passed you by,
A word, a phrase, someone else's daze.
You've felt its fury,
You've seen its mark,
It's touched your soul never to depart.

You've felt the panic, it smothers your mind
With images that won't let you unwind.
'I'll offer it up,' I've heard you say,
But why did it choose you in this way?

You remain strong on the outside,
Inside you cry.
For the lack of control, that comes out as why!

This lady who brought you life,
She's a mother and a wife,
She's a friend, a listening ear,
But now her eyes hold a fear.

Your approach to life will always bring hope.
Your presence, your light, will help her fight.
It's hard to be strong for one and all,
Sometimes it's like you're in freefall.

Hope for the future
Faith for today
My prayers are with you all the way.

Marie Hannon-McGee

Now What!

Life so far,
has been a struggle.
What lay ahead,
is such a muddle.

The children are all grown
now what do we do?
Retirement has come
and life should be new.

Hobbies are a must,
with time on our hands.
There's so much one can do,
if you sit and make plans.

Dry flower arranging for me,
and gardening for him.
Walks in the park,
just to keep trim.

More outings together,
should our pension stretch that far.
Free bus passes for us,
when all we want is a car.

We've served our country,
and family too.
Now come on Government,
what are we getting from you?

Susan Appleby

WHY?

Why? is a popular question in this world,
I first realised that as I *began* to fold

The clothes *he* left for *me* to iron last night,
Today *he* slapped *me* and told me to iron it right.

Y'see his underwear needs to be ironed, so precise, just right
I know I should say something, but I don't want to fight.

I thought the Homo sapien's supposed to be the modern man,
And now when he beats me, my mind's in another land.

At the beginning of this disturbed and violent relationship *he*
                                        promised *me* the earth,
The stars, the moon, gold, frankincense and myrrh.

Then suddenly everything started to change,
The loving man I once knew began to fade.

I knew *he* made a pact with the devil himself
When, one day, in a fit of anger he threw me across the
                                room and I crash-landed on the shelf.

'*Why* do you do this to me?' - I feebly cried
'I do it because *I love you*' - came the strange reply.

Why? is a popular question in this world,
He first realised this as *he* begins to fold

The clothes I left for *him* to iron last night,
So today I *punched him* and told *him* to iron it right.

Ayesha Lahai-Taylor

CAR BOOT SALE

It's all the rage, this day and age,
Car boot sales, in a field,
busy people milling round,
To see what they can yield.
Many things, layered in dust,
Fingerprints and grime,
Hustle, bustle, pull and tug,
'I saw that first, it's mine!'
Old cracked pots, packs of cards,
Net curtains, heaps of shoes,
Rusty spanners, socks and plates,
Bike wheel inner tubes.
Delving in a wooden trunk,
An ageing face looks up,
Smiling, and hoping to gain a sale,
Says 'Would you like this cup?'
Underfoot it's plain to see,
The rain's been beating down,
Ground sheets cover muddy grass,
To protect a dressing gown.
Children shouting, 'Oh! Look Mom,'
'This teddy, he's so soft!'
'Put it down dear, please don't touch,
There's plenty in the loft!'
When the boot sale's over,
And people drift away,
You can bet your bottom dollar,
They'll be back another day!

Diane Hendley

DAYS OF MY CHILDHOOD

Childhood days have all gone away
The years roll by but memories stay
Of years gone by I still recall
When fun was had by one and all
Life was easy then in so many ways
O how I long for those glorious days
When I would play with my friends from morning till dusk
And along with my friendship I gave them my trust
Then in my teens it was dancing and dates
Life was a ball for me and my mates
Along came marriage and I settled down
Washing babies' nappies to the Beatles' sound
Now I approach my twilight years
And along with old age come one or two fears
Big brother is watching
Mind what you say
Or the grim reaper will shortly be on his way.

Carol Murphy

MY BROTHER

It's always me in trouble
And not my little brother.
Whenever things start going wrong
He runs to tell my mother
And, somehow, it's always me getting into bother.

I didn't break his aeroplane,
I didn't hide his bat
And when you heard that awful screech,
It was he who squeeze the cat,
Not me - I wouldn't do a thing like that!

I never trip him over
Or sit upon his head.
That bump you heard upstairs last night,
'Oh' you will say 'Poor little Fred'
But I didn't kick him out of bed.

One day, perhaps, he'll tell the truth
And say it wasn't me,
Who ate the cake and broke the mug
And spilled the cup of tea.
'Til then I'll just put up with it
'Cos I like him, actually!

Linda Brinkhurst

THE TRIALS OF MOTHERHOOD

What a panic I am in,
The kids are at their tricks again,
He's hurt his leg, she's hurt her head
I do begin to live in dread
My hair's turned grey without a doubt
in fact I'm sure it's falling out
and trying to keep up their pace
is turning me into a hopeless case.

Oh no, one is missing, where can he be?
and gazing out of the window I see
a streaker flashing for all to see
his clothes in piles around his feet
A perfect cherub all complete.

The other one is very quiet and into the house I sped
to find my soap powder poured all over the bed
now to the television she sped
to jumble the colours blue green and red.

But later, when they are asleep
their little arms flung wide
I look down upon them
and my heart swells with pride,
and if anyone were to offer a million pounds or three,
I'd say no money in this world
could buy them both from me.

Shirley Smith

SEASONS

Swept along by blustery autumn winds
The leaves whirled past. My thoughts whirled too
As if beyond control.
Was this to be my autumn-time?
Like the leaves, was I
To have one last crazy dance
Before coming to rest in some hidden place?
Or would I, like the trees, bloom again
When you, my spring, returned?
You did not come. I walked alone,
Alone, alone, alone,
As the sun was sinking over our small town.

Beryl A Walpole

THOUGHTS FOR ST VALENTINE'S DAY

My sweetheart, darling, dearest one,
  My friend eternally;
What can I write? Love is such fun,
  And free, free, free.

Your voice is music to my ears,
  Your laughter I do miss,
Your lips can calm my deepest fears,
  So kiss, kiss, kiss.

As mighty as Niagara Falls,
  My love flows endlessly;
Forever constant, my love calls -
  It's me, me, me!

No height, no depth, can prove my love,
So fly, my love, and show
It's pure and white, just like a dove,
  And snow, snow, snow.

I've loved you, oh so long, my dear,
  My love will leave you never;
Let souls unite, my love is near,
  For ever, ever, ever.

Beryl Owen

THE EDGE OF TOMORROW

Close to the point where the land ends,
Where moon-touched cliffs cascade to sea,
While seabirds hover against the light,
Drawing, drawn to the edge are we.

Are we?
Or is it you and I?
Two ones or one two?
What would you say to stepping out into the elemental
Eddy below,
Risking grief or joy?

Below the foaming crash and swirl,
Silver, black, light and dark merging,
Behind us the surety of familiar land,
Ahead a world unknown.

Two strangers, chronologically,
Known to one another for forever
- and five and a half weeks -
Safe and warm on dry land.

If I step out into that spaciousness,
Will you step too?
Or will I, as I fall,
Turn to see you remain on the cliff?
Or shall I watch you lead, then fear to follow?
Either way, what then?

(We could keep safe and warm on dry land.)

Or if we go together,
Will the crashing waters far below engulf us?
Or, in stepping out in faith, shall we find
That we too, we two, take flight?

Or shall we stay safe and warm on dry land?

Sheila Hymas

THE WALL

The tank waits
Silent now
Gaunt and without purpose
A dramatic explosion of guns
Blasts the first way to freedom
After years lost behind concrete
A generation of suppression
Is turned loose
With no conception of the way forward
But to smash their way into the history books
With fragments of the wall
Crashing down all around them

High-pitched yells in foreign voices
And sweat from countless bodies
People are pushing, pushing forward
To the other side
Hands joining together through the opening
Creating a human chain of tears
Like slow motion puppets
With their strings untied
And mouths stretched to breaking point
In a generation of nameless faces

Camera bulbs are flashing
Capturing the moment for posterity
While overhead the flag of freedom
Ripples gently in the breeze.

Sylvia Ellen Mitchell

INFINITY

Consider the lily of the field,
Consider also the daisy,
A little face appears each dawn
To decorate a verdant lawn.
Insecticides and constant mowing
Will not prevent the daisy growing.
So when the darling buds of May
Burst forth in colourful array
Exotic blooms for the elite
As daisies crush beneath their feet,
Do not discount the daisy's power
Eternal life in one small flower.

Edwina Blackburn

MEN

Some darned men are just like bloody buses -
You wait around - for what seems almost a year -
As soon as one of them approaches your stop
That's when - two or three others appear

You look - and watch them - flashing their indicators
They are all offering - to take you on a ride
You're trying hard - to read the destinations
But - you haven't got much time - to decide

If you should turn your head even for just one second
It's too late - they've been - and now they've gone without you
Because there are so many options - at that other stop
They won't wait around - just for you - not for very long

Careful - catch one make a mistake - there's no turning back
Or - jump off - and you'll stand there puzzled - and gaze
While the taxis - cars and lorries - go whizzing by
Then also precious minutes - the hours - days and years.

Mary E Bridges

My Family Of Animals

I love my family of animals;
four dogs, two rats, one gerbil
plus two guinea pigs that can jig!
With all of these it is easy to see,
how I can never be lonely.

In all weathers I enjoy
walking my dogs in a convoy,
across fields, in woods,
or along a beach, anywhere is good.
Nowhere is beyond our reach.

Watching my rats being so active,
such pleasure to me they give.
The gerbil likes to burrow in sand,
such behaviour I can understand.
I love them all, the large and the small.

The guinea pigs softly squeak,
as I enter the room to me they speak.
'Come and give us a cuddle' they say.
Our moments together are the favourite time of day.
I love my animals throughout eternity.

At the close of day, for the night,
I turn out the bedside light.
Lay down my weary head,
the dogs and I, all in bed
until a new morn arrives at dawn.

E A Hicklin

I TRY NOT TO THINK

I try not to think,
of the way things used to be.
You at the end of the phone,
always pleased to see me.

I try not to think
of the time we spent,
being together with friends.
The letter you sent.

I try not to think
of what we had
or where we'd be,
if things hadn't gone bad.

I try not to think
of our feelings before.
How close we were,
but not anymore.

I try not to think
of the feelings you now share.
How happy you are without me,
I just pretend not to care.

I try not to think
how I could be so wrong.
I thought you loved me,
but now you're gone.

C D Townsend

Snapshots Of A First Grandchild

Perfect replica of human form
Blessed miracle you were born
Surpassing hope and expectation
Brand new member of our nation.

Wide, bright-eyed surveying all around
Suckling breast where true warmth is found
Child nestling close so calm and trusting
Small pink feet forever thrusting.

Rolling over on cushioned floor
Quickly turning back to roll some more
Anxious glances to parents near
Happy, gentle smiles to infant dear.

Baby chuckles hitting rattle
Infectious laughter, infant prattle
Firm, tiny fingers grasping hand
Welcome little person to our land.

Eve Stinson

ALL CHANGE?

All change, the picture's altered?
All change, fate takes a hand?
All change, a stronger power than us has very different plans?

All change, and how it matters?
Freedom was looming close
of sleepless nights and nappy creams
we'd had our fulsome dose.

All change, no foreign holiday?
No lazing by the pool?
All change, I'm feeling ancient,
and 'Must I look a fool?'

All change, and all depending on an unassuming stick?
And what is in the window when it's been wet a bit?
All change, and all anxiety, much pacing in the hall?
All change, when we'd been planning on having such a ball?

All change . . . ?
In fact - the answer's *No*.
Things are to stay the same.
And yes, I must confess, it really is a shame!

Anne Pratt

MY DAUGHTERS, MY LIFE

Did I give life to these wonderful gifts
Their beautiful faces with red rosy lips
How dainty and tiny and cuddly you are
The smell of my babies, my daughters, my stars.

Now I know a mother's love for it rushes through my veins
It's in the heart and in the blood, like the gentle summer rains
It ripples through my body and I'm not ashamed to say
The love I feel is special and it grows with every day.

Claire my beauty, my deep and moody one
Katherine the lovely and loyal little love,
Kirsty, what can I say - my sweet and gentle child
Three most precious angels that fill me with such pride.

How fast sometimes life slips by
I sit, I think, I often sigh
And I wonder what would I have done
If I hadn't had, my precious ones.

Caroline McKiverigan

UNTITLED

Wandering lonely as a cloud
Words that come to mind
They belong in a masterpiece
But I can't write that kind
I like a poem which details
Humour and emotion
And the ones with which lovers used to
Pledge their devotion
I like the ones which make you feel
This could be about me
The ones that are so true to life
Because they can set you free.

Grace Frackleton

LIFE IS SAD

Life is sad,
Life is sweet,
Life makes you happy,
Life makes you weep,
But 'Faith in your Heart',
You must always keep.

C Todd

ALICE

As I sit and watch her sleep,
Her fragile body old and weak,
Her legs too old to walk for long,
She often wonders what's gone wrong.
At 83 she's giving up,
She's the one who loved life so much,
Every day is just the same,
Up and washed and still the same.
She doesn't talk much anymore,
Waiting for that knock on the door,
To see a friendly face once more,
Perks her up, just once more.
There's no joy in growing old,
'Just keep going,' so she's told.

Pat Cheetham

THE DEPRESSION

Marching ghosts of long ago
Running through my mind
Faces only black and grey
No colour will unwind.

Never saw those stricken eyes
Or hollow hungry cheeks,
But dreams don't choose the ones they call
So I'm the one they seek.

Shuffling lines of shabby men
Drooping side by side,
Hunger's stolen manhood,
Handout's stolen pride.

Long should be forgotten,
Much of time's running sand,
But I can feel their sorrow
For now I understand.

Gwen Lewis-Watkin

WHO AM I?

I am a mother
That's for life
I was a wife
But for a short while
I am a person in my own right
But who am I?

M Oulton

UNTITLED

In times of trouble, hardship and woe
you feel, yourself where can you go?
Is there a light at the end of it all?
Is there a promise of happiness?
Perhaps any day this may change
as life becomes brighter, easier.
This alone comes from oneself
as you sit and think to yourself.
People know how you feel.
Let them help.
Make time for others to share your load.
The time you spend worrying
you could be thinking
of ways to help others and sort things out.
Be optimistic
and things will turn out,
you'll see.

Carole Gooch

LOST, ONLY TO BE FOUND

I wanted to love you, oh how I tried,
Year after year swallowing my pride.
You abused my trust, our daughter's too,
Now even our son is lost to you.

Those years I wasted, just rotting away,
But I've lived to see another day.

Bad times behind me, good times ahead
I've never felt better.
You're leaving my head.

With a long way to go
And a lot to do,
I'm finally feeling over you.

Fun and laughter, family and friends
I hope this feeling never ends.

Life's treating me well, the children too,
But what are you going to do?
You've lost it all, unfair you feel,
Life's dealt to you a crummy deal.

Once like a child so quiet and tame,
I'm feeling free to live again.
Growing, changing, determined to be
The person I've waited so long to see.

Angela Birch

IF I COULD FLY

I lie and gaze into the sky
Oh! how I wish that I could fly,
Far up high to clouds, like snow
Over land and sea I'd go.

Flying swift, flying free
Wondrous sights all new to me.
Swooping, diving, flying low,
Seeing nature's beauty glow.

Fields stretched wide in shades of green,
Seeing things I'd never seen.
Caught upon a gentle breeze
Then down to rest among the trees.

Up again towards the sun,
Feeling life has just begun,
Drifting, dreaming, not a care.
Peace and silence everywhere.

Head held high just like a king
I rise again with widespread wing.
Off to seek a new domain,
'Til summer comes, then home again.

Oh! how I wish that I could fly,
As I gaze into the sky.

Grace Wallace

MISSING YOU

These are the things which I think of when I miss you

The touch of your hand
The smile on your face
Your warm embrace
Things which I think of
When I'm missing you

These are the things which I think of when I miss you

Your gentle touch
As you brush my hair
The smell of you lying there
Things which I think of
When I'm missing you

These are the things which I think of when I miss you

Your warm sweep lips
As we tenderly kiss
Your big beautiful eyes
Things which I think of
When I'm missing you

These are the things which make you!

Sandra McDonald

ANGELS

It is cold and dark with no sun breaking free
I am cold and alone with no one to save me,
There are clouds in the sky and no birds up above,
There is hate in my heart with no room left for love.
I'm standing here alone at the place we first met
The wind is stinging my eyes, my cheeks are wet,
I think of the past and the times we have had
How could something so pure become something so bad.

I am sorry my love for what I have done
For stopping the time of one beautiful and young,
In life you were poor but now don't you see?
By releasing your life your spirit is free.
I close my eyes and in the dark I can see
I remember your face when you last saw me,
There was fear in your eyes but I saw it as love
I look at the sky and I see angels above.
As I step over the edge I know what's to come
I'm freeing my spirit and together we'll be one . . .

It was cold and dark with no sun breaking free
I saw them together but they didn't see me,
There was wind in my eyes and there were clouds in the sky,
As they stood there together I knew they would die.
As they moved towards the edge and went one by one
The clouds moved away and out came the sun,
There was nothing I could do and why should I try?
With angels above I knew they would fly.

Caroline Haycock

LAMENT OF THE SINGLE PARENT

Dreams shattered, cries unheard,
This single parenthood is hard to bear,
Struggling to make ends meet,
While catering to the patter of tiny feet.

Mum and Dad combine,
No time to be feminine!

So much to do
People sit in judgement
Of you.

Lost in confusion of what the world expects
When all we want is love and respect.

Has Women's Lib forgot
Superwomen we are not.

Anne McConville

IN LOVE!

I have been there . . . 'in love'
I have felt the hopes for the future,
and the fears of departure.
I've felt the loneliness of separation
and the excitement of the return.
The softness . . .
and sweetness of a 'together embrace'
has warmed and relaxed me.
Dreams were filled with
a loving future,
and nightmares . . .
of accidents on the way to work.
I have given and received
the surprise presents,
and shed tears of an anxious heart . . .
when it's ten minutes past 'home time'.
I've received the unexpected hugs,
and sometimes caught the 'watching' of me.
I've been content in the knowledge . . .
that I was . . . 'all that was ever wanted'.
I have been there . . . 'in love',
and I have the scars to prove it.

Alison Couzens

FISHING

Dan loved to go fishing on Fridays
Just to a nearby lake,
Sometimes there was so little action,
It was really hard, staying awake.
One day, a fisherman seated nearby
Was heard to shout, 'I've caught a big one!'
So, quick as a flash, Dan made a quick dash,
To watch all the action to land one.
The other man said, 'Hold my camera,
And take a photo of me and this fish.'
Dan neatly obliged and took four or five,
To make sure of him getting his wish.
'That's made my day!' said the fisherman,
'I'm going for a pint with my mates.'
So he packed up his rods, his bits and his bobs,
And off he went, through the gates.

Dan returned to his peg by the water,
There, a sorry sight met his eyes.
Two ducks had made a feast of his maggots,
And eaten up all his supplies.
They had made short work of his sandwiches,
And devoured the last of his flies.
Poor Dan had to pack up his fishing
And return home with nothing to show.
Still, he had seen a bit of the action,
As he related the tale to wife, Flo.
Said Flo 'Well, you helped him by taking a photo,
So you did your good deed for the day.
Come and sit down to your supper,
It's fish and chips, by the way.'

Connie Maltson

SAMARITAN

If you think all your friends have gone:
Think of me.
If all you want to do is run:
Run to me.
If you can't face the things you've done:
Turn to me.
If you've ran out of reasons to carry on:
Remember me.

Linda Hoult

JOURNEY TO HAPPINESS

Darkness surrounds me
There is no light,
The despair I feel,
I keep trying to fight.

You just get so tired
Of feeling this way,
Having to cope with another day,
But with each new day,
You carry on
The road to recovery
Seems oh so long.

Sometimes I think,
I'd be better off dead,
These are the thoughts
That I really dread,
But I know I'll get better,
You wait and see,
I'll look in the mirror
And say 'Hey that's me'
Where have you been (long time no see),
So to everybody who suffers like me,
Take each day as it comes
And think positively.

G Holzherr

JUST PAST TEN

The mine was in darkness, no sign of the men,
It was closed down yesterday just past ten,
It had been part of the village for many years,
Now all that was left were the family tears!

There'll be no money to pay the bills,
No more treats and no more frills,
The future looks bleak for all of the men,
With the closing of the mine just past ten!

Many of the wives just stand at the door,
Gazing and wondering as never before,
What of the future, what will it hold,
What other jobs can the village mould?

A community destroyed by the lack of work,
What other tremors around them lurk?
Their lives from now will be very humble,
The time's not far away when they'll start to grumble!

Their lifestyle gone never to return,
No glow from the fire, they have nothing to burn.
Confidence will be gone from all of the men,
With the closing of the mine just past ten.

The children will wonder and not understand,
As they walk down the street holding mother's hand.
They'll think of the times way back when,
Before the mine was closed, just past ten . . .

Joan M Crow

WOMAN

She is not a warrior
No metal, nor stone made her
Like a gentle breeze
She stimulates your mind
And nurtures your dreams
She is the other side of you
The dreamer.

Nicola K Todd